FLAME

Poetry Collection By
Angel Wood

∞

Pyramid Images
Atlanta, GA

ISBN 978-0981466095
PYRAMID IMAGES PUBLISHING, a division of Pyramid Images Inc.

1st Edition 2014

Printed in the USA

For my Eternal Flame, who showed me that real fire will not be contained, until we meet again, I remain.

ABOUT THE AUTHOR

Poet, playwright Angel Wood was born in Atlantic City, New Jersey. She moved into the projects of Dayton, Ohio with her family shortly thereafter. The Bella Vista Estates, where Angel called home, was a world of drug infestation and violence. It was a war zone and like any other war zone everybody leaves with scars. She had to deal with crack and heroine addiction in her own home, her family being torn apart, and her friends dying way too soon. Angel could have easily gone under with circumstance. Instead she chartered a new course, graduating high school with the highest grade point average in the city. She became the first person in her family to finish college, when she received her Bachelors Degree in Political Science and Criminal Justice from The Ohio State University. Angel started writing poetry very early in life as a way to express her thoughts and feelings. Poetry was a soul anchor for her as she navigated her way out of the projects. Even as gunshots rang outside of her bedroom window; Poetry offered an escape from the violence and confusion. With the pen Angel found her voice and with her words she hopes to give voice to those who have yet to find theirs. Angel's first book *A Spring in the Desert* has been very successful, many readers have reported finding strength in the truth of her words. In *Flame*, Angel delves into the human experience; powerful spirit confined in the flesh and the tension, friction, and passion that can ignite.

Table of Contents

Flame

The burning sands sifting away time

I grasp, as the grains run through

my chard fingers

did I dream you?

conjure you in my imagination

were you figment?

a passionate expression

of a fanciful impression

could this scorch be remnant

of my latent desire?

I crave an ethereal plume of heat

were you fire?

Black Magic

Black magic

Voodoo king

Casting a spell over me

I am seen

Blue fire

Heated torch

Searing your flame into me

I am scorched

Black lightening

Seeking Sun

Striking your force into me

I am done.

No Place Like Home

A triumph of years

A valley of tears

A still creek

Hidden by the brush

As the forest flames to ashes

A still beat of silence

Behind the tick

As a moment passes

The muscle beneath the skin

The marrow within the bone

Is Love

I may sail a thousand seas

In a hundred life times

But there is no place like home.

And Our Song

Purple roses fade to black

Giza stands in ruin now

Days do pass and none outlast

Except our song

Freedom to chains

Chains to broken clasps

Past secured in a book

Books to ash

But still remains our song

Overgrowth and industry

Tech expands to meet our needs

The more we see, the less we know

The more we have

The less we show

Distraction evaporating seeds to dust

Yet there remains us and

Our song.

Spark

Remarkable you

absorbing me

the way you do

igniting a flame

from a draft

got me craving

we outlast,

the brevity of our existence.

You have Remained

You have walked with me

these many miles

with your wings

you could have flown

far and wide

still you have remained

by my side

In life

you were a creature, wild

invincibly untamed,

screaming out f-the word,

uncaged

Roaring lion

with claws of blades,

And still, you have remained

with me

They feared you

because you were concrete,

your ways were hard

but I loved you

because you were just like me,

we shared the same scars

to me

you were tenderness

For me you were peace

the calm in my torrent

my lock, and my release

they called you a gangster

you choose the name thug

threatening black skin

beating a drum

of revolution

power poet,

uncompromising

calling forth

a ghetto uprising

unsung

written down in history

an angel,

Still, you have remained

with me.

The Box

Placing tenderness in a box

Beneath my bed

Chaotic trauma streaming

In the box inside my head

Paranoia locked

In the box

Beside my dresser

Darkest secrets told

In the box with my confessor

Walked the line within the box

Of my persistence

Bloodshot eyes stinging liver dry

Sucking the last drop

From the box of my existence

Pillow laid beneath my head

In the box of my resistance.

-For Amy Winehouse

September

Leaf blown promises

Strewn across my lawn.

Naked, I sit among

The midnight dusk

And wait for dawn

The smoldering heat

Has fled the night

Coolness settles in around

I run my fingers through the dirt

Then bury them deep

Into the ground

Dampness beads

About blades of grass

The porous soil

It has moistened enough

That the Earth opens up

And absorbs my past.

Woman, For Real

I love the fullness in my backside

The way I jiggle as I strut and glide

The sensuality in the thickness of my lips

The power grip in my thighs and my hips

I am a woman

A real woman, for real

Those boyfriend jeans wont fit me

Cause I bump and I bulge

I curve

I swoll

I got dump in my trunk

Too much to hold

Confined in a boy-cut

I am a woman

A real woman, for real

Let the super models keep that size two

I got something more betta for you

I be that Earth shaking

Got you contemplating

Future plans and baby making

Canceling b-ball cause I be your legs taking

Laying around in bed all day

Then a little late night brownie baking

Woman

For real

17

Adrift

Loneliness

a kite swept

by the wind

drifting

never ending

silence

when will love remain

with me?

and pass away the days

with me?

will I matter to anyone?

this aching, deft of anchor

this hollow, filled with rancor

is it to be soothed?

who can reach these heights

on which I am now carried away?

who will loose their cords and fly to me?

Afghan Girl

i cant feel my heart

but i study it,

examine it as if it were outside of me

It seems void

as a dark thing,

hidden inside of a black thing

while beating wildly in my chest

a fluttering caged bird

too terrified to scream

back bowed from my heavy load

purposefully unseen

when did this thing happen

that has turned me into a shadow?

griped me

held me fast, in my place

shrouded my face

made me into a ghost

who haunts in corners, and serves tea

i have soared somewhere before

i am sure of it,

freedom aches within my bones

and i ignore it

when i first burst through the womb

unaware of the rules

with all my dreams and things

21

flighty with joy, I'd dance and sing

until I was hobbled, fastened into place

put away in a corner

where dreams can not grow

kept in the dark

so my hopes could not show

soul locked in a cage,

innocence shut behind the door

I, the orchid

that would have bloomed in spring

is losing its leaves

for lack of tending.

Suffering

As it stares blankly into nothingness

Its eyes leek

Rage is pain too long contained

So much past pain it cannot speak

It does not notice the beauty around

So deep is that which ravishes it

In moments of quiet

Soon as the silence comes

It becomes undone

It believes there is a well inside it

That does not have a bottom

It feels as though there must be something

Inside of it that keeps swallowing its happiness

Before it reaches the surface.

It wonders how it is suppose to breathe?

Its tears spill from the eye and slide down the cheek

It thinks, why is peace eluding me?

Particles of Me

You emerged

From the ocean

I was sand

A tidal wave,

You rose

Above my plain

Falling upon me

You covered me,

Soaking me through

I swelled and filled

I absorbed you

With morning come,

You receded out

Into the sea

A torrent drawing

away with you

Particles of me.

Beneath The Drain

Lost beneath the blades of grass

A slithered, broken chard of glass

Assimilation of the mask

A fleeting, fitful, furrowed glance

A misting, wispy, flighty chance

The drumming low beneath the dance

A tune askew from corded sound

The battered, blasted, common ground

The thread that's missing from the lace

That forms a knotted home someplace

Sequential memories distorted

Gallant, graceful, unreported.

Turbulent, storming, flooding rain

Collects a pool beneath the drain.

Lost in You

I could lose myself in you

Vanish in the fold of your embrace

You, could erase me

Sever me from concrete

Detangle me from the tangible world

I in you a vaporous steam

A disintegrating particle of light

A fleeting dream

I could lose myself in you.

The Cycle

After the storm

Has torn the core

Worn bare trust

Emaciated hope

Settled the clouds

To dust

The Quiet remains

Apart from pain

Absent of blame

In hallowed ground

Soaked with rain

A seed sprouts

Its promise

Again.

Remembering Trayvon

They said set fire to the rain

pain and rage mixing

in a thunderous cage

I suppose could ignite a mighty blaze

but what about love denied?

or trust defied? as

Neighborhoods Watch

blood shed dried

then swept away

covered over with prejudice

and Standing Ground.

turning cheeks

32

leading

to stinging necks

and

knots that tighten

from the strain of

"one time too many"

AND...

"that could have been my baby".

-For Trayvon Martin (Feb 5, 1995-Feb 27, 2012)

Worn

You are the lyric unwritten

Song, unsung

Peace beneath the gaping hole

All that is left undone

What is a thing that seems concrete?

A bridge to nowhere, where ends unmeet

When all that falls away, is you

I face myself in a space, untrue

Nestled deep between the thorns

The nectar of a dream unborn

Tattered shards of threads I've worn

Disintegrate as if never sewn.

When We Were

I recognize the recollection in your eyes

Of a moment, outside of time

When our souls were so intertwined

Before our stubbornness bore mountains

Our pride shifted into Continents

Or our tears pooled into oceans

Before our positions became religions

Or our egos went forth as lightening and starting striking

And the thunderous quakes, shook away remembrance

We were one

Before there were need of bridges

Or solar towers to communicate

35

We did not see Eye to Eye, we were the same I

Before our intent fragmented into language

And we lost ourselves in this world

Before our fear became politic, or our nuances war

We were one.

Black Bird

Black bird

Singing your song

Before the world

Light shining in a black wound

Sound resounding in a vacuum

Giving pieces of pieces

Yet no peace for you found

Black bird, wings drenched

In the bathtub drowned.

-For Whitney Houston

Dear Love

Circumstance

clipping at my heels

trying to fly,

soar to new horizons

yesterday reminding me

that I should be crawling

providing for me

past images of me falling

determinedly I flap,

struggling to stretch

imagining the wind

beneath my wings

but now my cuts, have opened up

they burn and sting

if I could just get to that place

which could erase

the damages imprinted on my mind

If I could just outpace

all former disgrace

leave every trace behind

but my thorns

are made of stone

they've burrowed deep

into the bone

not only do they prick

and bleed

but the weight,

impedes

my flight

to you.

Blue Star

Blue star

Spitting sparks

In the backseat of a

Hired car

A stage coach

Shuttling through

The universe

Every step a stage

Thousands crowd

Wishing on a blue star

Flaming to ignite

And incinerate the cage.

New York City

Subway, buses, bricks to brownstone

Cramp quarter living, and still alone

Summer's heat sizzling the pavement

December wind blasting around corners of the financial

district

Heads down, walking stride quick with determined steps

Mantra on repeat...Gotta get there.

Where?

Everywhere.

We all came here to get there.

Harlem with its barbeque and Renaissance history

Brooklyn's Bed-Stuy, a taste of little Italy

The Village and the parks,

But not the parks after dark

New York, the insomniac's city

Not enough shelter to house the many.

Because we all came here to get there.

Where?

Everywhere.

We all came here to get there.

Truth Alone

Spent all this time Rejecting

When I was meant to be

Accepting

Trying to plug up my own hole

While my own soul I was neglecting

At all cost protecting my heart

From the remembrance of Loved depart

The consequence Evasion

And all the phony Imitations

Just here to toy with.

The Lie spies I

And seeks to destroy with its one weapon, Illusion.

44

If I let the strike stick and fall into Delusion

Or chase away Truth until it hides in seclusion.

I will have lost more in this life than I had spared to give.

More of my good fortune

Than I had cashed to live

And even if I, high on the hog in my Delusions,

Circle the dance floor of fog with my Illusions,

While Evasion hosts a champagne toast to Lie

And all the Imitations raise their glasses high.

Still the day will come,

When all's undone, and I am just one,

With the Truth alone.

The Great Oak

raising daisies

listening to all that jazz

remembering yesterdays

preludes of the hourglass

the sands draining through

the evergreen

glistening moonlight

trapped beneath the lake

46

bending to the whistling wind

swaying towards the break .

Isis and Osiris

You are an ancient beauty

We are and ancient love

You were torn asunder in many pieces

Hidden away from me

And I walked the realms to find you

To gather you unto me

Flesh cannot live separated from bone

And Isis cannot breathe without her home,

Osiris, we are one

You became my Solomon

And I Sheba, Queen of Ethiopia

I heard tale of your wisdom and I was astounded

I burnt offerings of sweet incense in praise

That once again I had found him

The poet and the prince

My most precious stones

Jade, Gold, Diamonds, Obsidian, I gave in tribute

Your councilors rebuked me for my tradition

When from well before the beginning of time

It was you who were my religion

I have been written down in countless tale

None of which hold true

I am said to have served so many gods

But I have worshiped none but you

Do you recognize me Osiris?

It is I, Isis

You have been hidden from me again

Yet, I will find you

Powerful the force of our passion splintered the

Foundations of Gaia

Your caress sent shivers that shook the heavens loose

The stars fell like rain into the Mediterranean Sea

That night you lit the moon

To get a better look at me

Then, our love was rendered Treason,

Somehow we, were at war

But still I could not help myself,

The soul is without reason

To be without you, I could not bear it

There is no world I wish to walk without us two

To share it

But they ran me through with swords for it

Till I bled dry upon the floor for it

But before my spirit flew, there were you

Do you recognize me Osiris?

It is I, Isis

You have been hidden from me again

Yet, I will find you

You came in through Palestine

I moved to Tel Aviv when I was three

I boarded the bus like I normally do

It was two stops down when I saw you

Your hands were in your pockets

It was cold and your jacket was threadbare

Your eyes were to the floor

And it was all I could do not to stare

How beautiful you were, Osiris

Even absent your royal fare

Even as vacant as you were right there

You lifted your eyes for a moment

And in that moment they met mine

I saw you,

A pit of sorrow, before the blast

Then we both slipped out of time

Osiris

Don't you recognize me?

It's me, Isis

You have been hidden from me again

But, I'll find you.

Blind

Talking a good game

Fraudulent, funny faces

All the same

Covering up

that that won't shine

obliterated self

Blind leading the blind

54

Little Girl in the Window

She opened up the window shade

Sat there upon the wooden seal

To see the view that God had made

She had to keep there very still

A rumble grew within the house

Voices raised, chaotic screaming

Get down from there you trifling louse

And put away your useless dreaming

She could not stay upon the ledge

Would not return into the dread

She swung around her tiny legs

Jumped down and darted straight ahead

What a Waste

What a waste

It would have been

Had I not had

Courage enough to stand

What a waste

It would have been

To spend all my life to fit in

Voting with the populace

Wearing the pre-cut rags

Fitting my round

Into the cone

Labeled

And search engine tagged

In the end

What a waste

It would have been

To not be

Me.

Auntie's Pearls

Sometimes

I feel

Like I was born

In the wrong time

Rather be sitting

On the stoop

Getting my scoop

Instead of

Text Me

Tweet Me

Follow Me

Like Me

All this false connecting

In the intangible space

Of Cyber world

When all I want to do

Is Harlem Swing

In Auntie's pearls.

The Breakup

blasted

trauma

potholes

in

my

lawn

tears

over

eggs,

eggs

over

easy.

Paris

As I long

for you now

I remember

you are within me

always

as I was once

within you.

Wisdom

I wasted my youth

With rambling things

On hearts with wings

That soared

In all different directions

If I could choose

To do my days again

I would anchor myself

To you.

Mid Night Recollection

Settling down

at night

in the quiet

when all else

is done

I remember

that I love you.

Imagine Me

Imagine me

Perched in a gilded cage

Content in a spot you picked

Nestled

On the outer edge of your life

Chirping

Your favorite melody

Waiting for you

To come play with me.

Then...SNAP OUT OF IT.

Not gonna happen.

Malcolm's song

I got tired of hiding

Wanted to walk out in the sun

Bravely, I met my day

One soul amid the guns.

-For Malcolm X

Drowning Doubt

Listening to the cymbal crack

Afterwards a silence comes

After words there comes the knot

Symphonies of dread

Occupying space meant for

Thoughts of...

U can be anything

Instead replaced with something said to U

Before U could remember

And it stuck there

It is stuck there, still...

U play your music really loud because of it

Trying to drown sound

from a place that cannot forget.

Hip Hop

Twist the dial up real high

Blasting base

Till trouble trembles

And shatters

Beneath the Treble

Like S dot Carter

Them woofers make the song cry

Beat pounding in my chest

Keepin my eyes dry.

Either Or

stuffed into a box

limbs secured

and tied in a knot

mouth taped shut

with that silver duct

OR

living free

within my self

on the wings of thought

I range beyond

that which is expected.

The Temptation of Jazz

He came blowin all that jazz

Tootin his horn

And strikin all the right keys

I swear,

If I wasn't tied to the blues

That boy might coulda played with me.

Inelegantly

She got out the best way she could

Inelegantly

She burst forth through the window

Tore down the shade

Inelegantly

She had sat and planned her way

To do her part

As a lady with etiquette and elegance

She would take her start

But as she patiently waited for perfection

To arise

For the appropriate occasion

To take the lead

Time continued passing

The manicured precision

Of indecision

Held her stagnate

And she had to break free from it

It wasn't pretty, but she did it

Inelegantly

Her hair was messed,

Her clothes were torn

Her pockets to pence

But she, reborn

Couldn't afford to stay cute

The world could not endure she stay mute

Might of stumbled her words,

But she spoke

Not even sure where the steps would lead,

But she'd go

Could not stay put in seclusion

Tucked away in her comfortable piece

Of delusion

As outside the walls were tumbling down

She'd walk the ground now, even if there

Was just rubble beneath her feet

To follow the path, even as it leads

Inelegantly.

Technicolor Dreams

Technicolor dreams

dripping from my alabaster box

the consistency of melted cream pops

sticky as it over flows the top.

I see all sorts of things as I peer

into my Technicolor dreams

Palm trees dance the hula dance

waving in the breeze

the oil drains from pelican wings

and flows back into the sea

as a Technicolor green

His smile my favorite turquoise blue

My neon yellow sun, it sears into

We blast a purple diamond cut

the glint I swear

Could blind me with its glare

if not for that shaded brown chair,

over there, in the corner of my

Technicolor dreams.

Into Me See

Peer into me

pierce through my shell

I am naked before you

hidden desires, laid bare

I retreat into the hollow

where I am self-contained

still somehow you follow

and navigate the maze.

The Noise

The noise

The static

The chaotic chatter

Yesterday's news

Playing

A reel displaying that gone,

Never to come

The much left undone

Quiet resting

Still

Beneath the disturbance of peace

Absence in reality

Of anything

That matters

Manifesting unnoticed

Beneath the shattered fragments

Of thought

I project I

and into the mangled self is caught

There is nothing really

There is nothing really

Reality is nothing really

A mirage, a homage to captive me

Whose belief in the dream

Causes me to scream

When the illusion is shattered

As if I could be shaken

But can a concept break?

Can a thought be torn to pieces?

Can the Divine reflection

Of Eternal Light wither and die?

The tears that slip from my eye

An evaporating mist

Are just literary conventions

In my plot twist.

Remembering Yesterday

Yesterday I cried for the mistakes I have made

For the turns I missed

I cried for the ones that I looked past,

that needed just a moment of my time

For the ones that I neglected to see

while they were right in front of me

Yesterday I cried for the loves

that I will never hold again

the voice I can no longer hear

Yesterday I cried

for the ones who died

before I remembered

how much that I loved them

I cried for what I cannot undo

for what I failed to do

I cried because that was all I could do

I asked God if my tears meant anything to Him,

if He acknowledged them?

If they were considered prayer?

These tears came from such a depth

Yesterday I cried from my soul,

the tears welled up from a place in me

the core of me

they formed a pool in the cradle of my eyes

And one by one slid down my face with purpose

Like the purpose in a prayer.

Proclamations of Black

Proclamations of black

Within the revelations of coal

Shiny dust fabric

Once laced in gold

Melodies over flood

Abbreviations over love

As time danced in the flame

Unaware.

Brevity

I close my eyes

and I remember

how your eyes

laughed and burned

at the same time

and how your smile

could penetrate ice.

How Much You will Love Me?

I rise like the sun

Your eyes follow me

Each passing moment

On wings, am I esteemed so high

Desired, wanted so,

I fly

You say that I am beautiful.

I lift... Beautiful how?

Just then I do soar

See, I'm beautiful now

You are drawn to me, and I to flight

My capture becomes your fervent plight

How will you contain me?

Plan to wait till I nest

Cast your net and restrain me?

I'd shiver with fear in the palm of your hand

You'd stroke at my nape till I'm calmed again

Sit me in your golden cage

Shut tight so I won't fly away

Clip my wings ensuring that I stay

Is that how much you will love me?

Enough to see the light within my eyes

Tarp my cage, because I shine too bright

Fearful, I might escape and soar

Spirit, trying to dim it just a bit

Hoping I'll forgot about flying

And sit

Is that how much you will love me?

Echo of a Psalm

Lace, delicately crafted on a prayer

beautifully blended

light as air

rising on a cloud

dancing on a waking dream

gold dust sifting through the palm

a feather on a stream

the echo of a Psalm.

Where Angels Meet

Far above the clouds

There we are

Joined beyond the day

Outside the grasp of gravity

Are we

Afloat on fulfilled promise

We shed our wings

Along with all the countless dreams

We have dreamed

And there rest, in stillness

Where atmosphere cannot reach us

We smile that knowing smile

And shake the stardust from our feet

Then recline on that Sacred Rock

Where angels meet.

The Pinnacle

I have walked,

a thousand trials

Swam,

a thousand tears

climbed,

a thousand fears

I will not be removed.

www.ingramcontent.com/pod-product-compliance
Lightning Source LLC
Chambersburg PA
CBHW071354090426
42738CB00012B/3116